REAL SITUATION

In a world of lies and confusion, where do you begin to know life? Where do you begin to get over the hurt and pain; lies told to you again and again? So you cross your fingers whilst continuing to linger; deceive.

What may be life to you is death to some and this is the sad part. We are so conditioned to accept lies that no matter what you try, you cannot filter it out of your life.

Yes this is sad but this is the life we live. We live in a world where life and or people has and have become corrupt; not valued, sold short.

Thus what is life if life is worth naught?

Michelle

As I look forward to a new year, I look forward to throwing away my old baggage. Look forward to starting anew with full and total truth not just in my life, but with Lovey and the true and good seeds he has and have given me.

I look forward to a better tomorrow for me and my family; children including Lovey and my gorgeous mother.

I look forward to the day when earth will once again have true peace and harmony and is void of all sin and evil including wicked and evil people, animals and spirits.

I look forward to hope; a new hope that spells true peace in my life.

As I look forward to 2016 and beyond, I leave my past behind and start anew; fresh, in goodness and in truth.

All that fail me and cause me pain and hurt; I truly let go and walk in my truth and freedom; care.

I leave all the negative and evil packages and baggage of God and family behind and create a new world that is clean for me and only me. Yes this is selfish on my part but in truth, if you are evil and negative, I truly do not want or need you around me or in my world of goodness and truth; freedom. Life is not restrictive thus I want and need no restrictions in my good up, good up life.

Negative and evil forces truly have to go without end.

As 2015 come to a close, I leave behind a God that has truly failed me and I cut ties with him infinitely and indefinitely. No, I can't leave Lovey. He won't let me leave him and this is fine despite me saying I am slowly leaving him. What I need though; is to recharge me and get my health and mind together where I am not living a restricted life. I cannot relive the past nor do I want to. All I can do now is make better choices for me and only me. Yes you and my family because in truth, I cannot do without the good and true seeds Lovey has and have given me.

I cannot continue on in pain and financial hardship; so I leave all that keep me back in life behind and move on to a better and more prosperous life and future for me and yes you. Without goodness you cannot have truth and without truth you cannot have goodness come on now.

I cannot stay stuck in an environment that cause me pain; thus I've come to the conclusion that no god whether good or evil is good for me. Truth isn't about pain, but yet I've found more pain than truth in my life. I've found sorrow, longing, injustice, death and so much more and this is truly sad. Life; true life, isn't about hurt or pain like I've said nor is it about death, it's about truth; true truth.

It's amazing how we see certain things and know certain things but we are just stuck in the past or in the same old same old. Yes we all have different situations, but why do we have be stuck? Just yesterday I was in tears due to my situation in life. I want and need to leave Canada but I am *stuck here. Winter plays havoc on my body at times and this year my body so cannot take the cold; not even for a hot minute, but I am bearing on. So I was in tears and I went to sleep and this young and beautiful black female was comforting me in my great grandmother's house. She was hugging me and I began to cry whilst telling her I am so not looking forward to my 50th birthday. See people, I was so excited that I am reaching a milestone in my life. I am going to be 50 real soon. I was even telling my sister I am so looking forward to being half a century and she thought I was weird. I truly look forward to getting older people but yet yesterday I just lost it emotionally. In the dream I was not afraid to sleep in my great grandmother's home, but I was afraid to sleep in my grandaunt's home; house. I tried going into the end room of my great grandmother's house but a wall was there and I could not get through it. I was stuck. I tried again to go through that pathway and the same wall came up and I was stuck, could not go through that pathway. There was another pathway for me to go but suitcases with clothes was blocking my pathway; so there is a blockage in my pathway and I am so tired of it. Is my family blocking me from what I want and truly need to do? I truly don't know, but I am being blocked all around and I am truly tired of it.*

Yes I-Octane was in the dream. He was in my grandmother's house and he was telling me about a television show he did here in Toronto and how the host was a snob; stuck up and offish I guess. He told me the lady's name but I can't remember it; thus the dreams in a dream that I am having as of late.

Dreamt about the current Jamaican Prime Minister, Portia Simpson Miller. The dream had to do with Andrew Holness and his 250 million dollar mega mansion he's building in Beverly Hills Jamaica. I think I asked her in the dream where Andrew Holness got the money from and she did not know.

People, mi affi ask wey di $250 million dollars come from?

JAMAICA AND THE PEOPLE OF JAMAICA ARE STRUGGLING AND YU MEAN TO TELL MI SEY, DISYA MAN YA HA $250 MILLION DOLLARS JAMAICAN FI SHELL OUT PAN OUSE SOH?

The question flags and marks are going up. A soh eee pay fi bi Prime Minister or a former Prime Minister of Jamaica?

Well den mi affi run fi a seat den.

<u>Yu a government official an ha dat dey kine a money?</u>

There are so many people in Jamaica that $250 million could have fed. Look pan Riverton how people a live inna dump; literal dump lan wey garbage truck dump rubbish inna; an yu a goh tell me sey, disya man ya ha suu much money, an im couldn't help di people dem inna Riverton?

A soh wi tan?

Bumbleet to kakka caunna to yass.

Man, 250 million dollar ouse an pickney caan fine food fi nyam; eat?

Some parents can't fine food fi put pan table.

Some people are dying of and or for medical want and need including shelter, and yu a goh bill a 250 million dollar fortress inna Jamaica?

People dey pan eee street homeless and yu a goh slap dem inna dem face like this?

Wow, dis a heavy load to carry to yass. Hence Jamaica truly has no hope and the window of Lovey is closed to all of you literally.

Wow because the selfishness of our own is beyond me. You know the plight and situation of some a di people dem out dey an yu a goh du diss to dem?

Wey eee money come from?

No, I should not have to ask because we all know and the global community all know sey, every politician inna Jamaica a scamma, rabba; thief an murderer. Thus some a unnu fren dem wey did dey inna army an police force that carried out illegal killings are hiding out in Cuba, Canada, England, the United States, Cayman and other countries across the globe. Every Jamaican know this, but are afraid to talk because snipers dey bout fi X dem out of life. Thus death take by any means necessary. Malcolm X

Oh to regile. Mi figet sey unnu did sign a deal with England to allow a prison to be built in Jamaica and they, the government of England handed over money to unnu. Also, I did read where the European Union gave unnu money for buggery, so yes unnu a ha field day with free money whilst the Jamaican People will have to pay fi unnu greed shortly.

Wow because di people dem fool fool yu si. None did the math of having this prison in Jamaica. If it costs $10 million Pounds; British Pounds per year to house and or keep these Jamaican prisoners in prison in the UK, how is Jamaica going to maintain and sustain them to meet international standards? Jamaica ha datdey kine a money dey fi house dem? Oh yeah, di IMF didey fi beg a loan; handout because eee seem dat a wha Jamaicans good fa. Lang han and beggy beggy to rass. Wi come eeene lacka fire truck to rass. Doesn't say much about us does it.

As of December 09, 2015 one British Pound is equivalent to $181.97 Jamaican Dollars. Now do the calculation and tell me if Jamaica has this kind of money to pump into a jail and or jail system each and every year.

I got $1, 819,700000 for a figure.

Oh wait, mi figet di new world order that the devil's society is trying to implement.

Ah yes, the joys of slavery. And I am being sarcastic people because given the current situation of Jamaica and if Jamaica doesn't sink; I can see slavery taking fold globally again. DI JAMAICAN PEOPLE DEM A GOH HAFFI WUK AN HAN OVA EVERY PENNY TO DI GOVERNMENT FI PAY DEM BILL. So yes Jamaicans will be working for free whilst dem pickney dead fi hungry just fi pay off di debts their so called joyous politicians put dem inna.

Kakka faate, fi goh si di pickney pan mamma back inna massa field again. Some a dem a goh haffi wuk inna di fields from before dem come outta belly to claate. <u>Thus all that our freedom fighters fight for was all for naught BECAUSE A TRUE NIGGAS OF THE WORST KIND SELL US OUT AGAIN.</u> All humanity have to do is look at the global population and see which nations are the most corrupt and vile; worse off financially right now. See the black nations and where they rank?

Does this tell you anything? But yet we stand up and proudly say we created it all; built civilization. Please, the black population have become the joke of many nations globally. Instead of taking a good look at self; we've become followers not leaders. We complain about so much including the mistreatment of others; us, but in truth, **WE TRULY DO NOT SEE HOW WE TREAT OUR SELF; OWN.**

We do not see our corrupt leaders that are mistreating our people, the resources and the country they claim to govern and or oversee. Just take a look at Africa and what Africa has and have become because of our black own.

Look at the Caribbean **especially Jamaica** and other islands and see **how our black own mistreat and rob their black own.**

We do not see the beauty of life Lovey has and have given us, but yet we claim to be black; are the original creation.

We as a people have become warped; ungrateful because all that our freedom fighters have and has done for us; we've disgraced them, and in truth none truly remember them. Look at our black societies today and truly tell me what did they die for?

What have we become as a people and race; nation?

Have we not regressed backwards?

Have we not lost our self respect and values?
Blackness

<u>Are we not promoting the devil's agenda instead of preserving and maintaining black truth?</u>

Thus the black nations of the globe have and has become powerless; the vagabonds and slave owned of this world.

We have no shame; thus we are the truly hunted. We have no rights in this world, the world we built; created.

We've become slaves (Abdullah's) to all on earth. We all know this, but instead of capitalizing on our truth and culture we let others demean it including us.

There is truly no black worth anymore because millions bleach their skin, tattoo their skin to be a part of the gangs of death, many distort and disgrace our nappy and happy as pappy black hair, many abandon their children even sell and kill them. ***<u>Thus all the life we were given, we as a race and nation; people have and has destroyed it literally.</u>***

Because of this destruction, ***<u>WE AS A RACE AND PEOPLE TRULY DO NOT KNOW WHO AND WHAT WE ARE.</u>*** ***<u>So we squabble about hue; the light skinned and dark skinned bullshit and or agenda.</u>***

Knowing all of this Lovey, you have the Gaul to tell mi bout Superman last month. Yu nuh real or just are you God and or Lovey? How can anyone have justice in a lawless society? Come on now. **When you let others take away our knowledge and truth what do we have left as a nation and people?**

Are we not left with lies and deceit?

Will we not live in lies and deceit and do wicked and sinful things?

Nothing can survive without truth. You and I know this, but yet you let humanity be deceived by wicked and evil people. Yes I know your truth and you cannot live with the unclean. I get it, **but why give 24000 years when you knew billions would turn against you and deceive you. The devil offered and billions accepted without truly thinking of you Lovey come on now.**

TRULY TAKE A LOOK AT THE REAL SITUATION OF EARTH AND THEN COME TALK TO ME WITHOUT YOUR BULLSHIT PERIOD.

NO GOD THAT IS REAL AND TRUTHFUL WOULD LEAVE THEIR CHILDREN IN UNDESIRABLE SITUATIONS COME ON NOW. Our situation here on earth is real, thus Bob Marley told us in his song REAL SITUATION and the title of this book. No, I did not want to join the two but I have to.

He, Bob Marley told us, **_"there ain't no use no one can stop them now."_** You the people of earth basked in the delicacies of the devil without thinking that **ALL THAT THE DEVIL HAS AND HAVE DONE IS TO DESTROY YOU.**

THE MORE WE SIN IS THE LONGER OUR SPIRIT STAY IN HELL BEFORE IT DIES. EACH SIN ACCUMULATE, THUS THE VALUE OF ONE IS NOT 24000 YEARS BUT 48000+ YEARS.

SOME SINS ARE AUTOMATIC DEATH; THUS DEATH CAN SAY BECAUSE YOU DID THIS, THE VALUE OF YOUR SIN IS NOT 48000+ YEARS BUT INDEFINITE YEARS.

Not one of you know that there are no rules in hell because Hell is not life but death and Death rules the underworld.

Billions of you are going to become slaves to Death and if you think slavery on earth was anything; you had better think again because it's worse in hell. **_WE WENT AND OR YOU WENT AGAINST TRUTH; LOVEY, SO YOUR PUNISHMENT WILL BE MORE THAN YOU CAN BEAR DAY IN AND DAY OUT IN HELL._**

Oh and knowing death, **DEATH CAN SAY, ONE DAY WILL BE MORE THAN A THOUSAND YEARS. DEATH CAN MAKE ONE DAY 48000 EARTH YEARS.**

SO TRULY THINK BECAUSE THE LIFE YOU SAVE WILL BE YOUR TRUE OWN.

Just yesterday I said; I truly don't care, we (Lovey and I) are over forever ever and I am going home and see yu sen di young lady to comfort me in my hour of need and you put up blockage and stoppage so that I cannot return home.

You are blocking me from going to Jamaica not my family. So now tell me, if you can block me from going home, why can't you elevate me prosperously and financially?

Why are you not blocking all that is wicked and evil from reaching our good and true own including me come on now?

There are things that can be done here on earth for the better Lovey because I know you are the way. <u>So why are you not doing it?</u>

Why do you continue to let corrupt systems and people stand; continue to govern and or rule over humanity; this earth and universe including spiritual realm?

You keep showing me your way, but yet I am lonely and depressed, no longer looking forward to my coming of age. I know you are not going to do anything special for me *because this is truly you; thus I am on my own this December.*

I even asked you, what was the point of me writing the book WHAT ABOUT DECEMBER if you are truly not going to listen to me and do anything for the betterment of this earth, me, our true and good family, my children and my family; those who are truly dear to me?

Also Lovey, why let her join me to him?

Do I not value cleanliness, so why him and not someone else?

Why should I be unhappy with you and why should evil continue to wreak havoc here on earth and in the spiritual realm and universe?

Why should my life be stuck in the dark ages; the old?

I need a new state of mind and you truly cannot give me this true and clean state of mind.

I've failed in all I've done and see; now my books cannot go out on time due to a glitch in Lulu's system. So why do I bother when all I get is disappointment; failure? And truly don't tell me disappointment is for a reason because I've been disappointed all the days of my life and it seems; it cannot stop. So yes, I constantly complain to you because you're all I've got.

I truly want out Lovey. No, not to live a dirty life but to live a clean life with me and me alone now. I am truly tired of failure and I am truly tired of failing with you.

No, I truly do not want or need another god. I just don't have any more fight left in me. Health is shot this month and you see how the cold is wreaking havoc on my body. So no, you cannot hear me and I am tired of crying; so I have to do me now.

And no people, another god never entered my thoughts and or mind. <u>IT'S JUST PLAIN OUT NASTY AND DISRESPECTFUL; DISGUSTING PERIOD.</u>

I have to live for me because at the end of the day, neither life or death is truly good for me.

One cannot have life without truth. And Lovey, all you've given me truly did not pan out; so we both failed each other in some way.

Yes people live and kill for death. I see this each and every day but as of yesterday Lovey, things are different between us and I am truly glad. Maybe now you can find someone to truly love you the way you wanted and needed to be loved. To me, my true love is truly not what you needed nor could you grasp or comprehend my true truth; good and pure; clean heart. I am truly different from you and in many ways too clingy. But I truly love clingy, thus I cling to you so much and I guess you did not like that.

Yes I bug you and tell you I am leaving you a lot and that you truly did not like even though I am smiling writing these words.

In truth, I guess I was never important to you in that way. I was just another pawn to you. Your lies worked; so truly thank you for teaching me about fathers. When you truly need them they are not there. Only mothers are there thus I saw the beautiful young black female comforting me. ***Yes I am grasping at straws with the fathers bit, but you know it's me.*** ***Thus this fiscal year is coming to a close and I have to truly clean out all the dirt in me that is left in my closet.***

Had to go there Lovey and in truth, truly forgive me because I am so not trying to piss you off in any way.

Yes it's time for us to come to the end of our journey Lovey and begin a new one based on full and true truth from the get go. Well we had that, I just need good and positive changes for us here on earth as of January 01, 2016. ***SO AS I DEDICATE COMING IN FROM THE COLD BY BOB MARLEY TO US, LET'S NOT FORSAKE EACH OTHER ANYMORE. LET US UNIFY IN GOODNESS AND IN TRUTH, TRUE PEACE AND HONESTY, HARMONY, CLEANLINESS, TRUE AND GOOD LOVE, TRUE WEALTH AND HEALTH; PROSPERITY FOR THE GOODNESS OF US AND ALL THE GOOD PEOPLE AND SPIRITS AROUND US.***

Lovey as I lift your head up smile and not be so sad like me.

Come on, it's time we come in from the cold and warm each other up.

Let good and true life be ours for real more than forever ever without end.

So, truly let me find a way for the both us to live good and true. **_We need each other because without truth we have not life literally._**

Without truth; all we have is death, *and in truth, I truly don't want to die. I need good and true life; thus I truly need you despite me saying I am slowly leaving you.*

So open your doors and windows; home to me so that we can live come on now.

No more lopsided relationships Lovey because it's truly not healthy. Too dysfunctional and I truly don't want or need our dysfunctional relationship to continue. We need a healthy relationship. So as of December 29, 2015 on your day, let's forgive each other and throw away our dysfunctional relationship and begin a new with a healthy one. My spirit needs this healthy relationship with you Lovey so that we both; (flesh and spirit) can truly live.

Michelle

REAL SITUATION

How do I find my way on this day Lovey?
How do I find my way with you?

Talking does not work between us.
Listening is not your strong suit and all I see is disappointment in my life with you.

I can't even talk anymore because I have to truly wonder if you see the real situation here on earth?

<u>I cannot fathom why you would allow men; wicked and evil people to stockpile weapons of more than mass destruction to kill?</u>

Look at the weapons of death here on this earth Lovey and tell me if this is what you wanted for humans?

Are all these weapons of mass destruction and diseases necessary; needed Lovey?

When did we as humans get so vile and evil Lovey that we have to destroy the life of humans; self, trees, plants, and animals, the waterways of life; the earth and universe?

The situation is real and critical here on earth but yet you don't see this Lovey.

Yes I want and need all facets of evil to leave earth more than infinitely and indefinitely forever ever without end, but I am out voted due to the wickedness and evils; sins of man, humanity here on earth, in the universe and spiritual realm.

Mother Earth I have to ask, was this what you wanted for self; life here on earth?

I've talked to Lovey, but I've never truly talked to you to find out how you feel as to how humans treat you and kill you. Do you not care for self; you?

Do you not cry; grieve to see that you provided a home for humans and we've destroyed you?

Where is justice, true justice when it comes to you?

Why do you even permit different countries to stockpile their weapons and diseases of more than mass destruction and more than inhumane cruelty in you?

So then, the saying is true, if evil cannot have it all they are going to destroy it all. Now I ask you, if you know the truth of life, why continue to give wicked and evil people and lands a home in you and in the universe?

Why not unify in truth and harmony; true peace and cleanliness; goodness and truth with Lovey and all that is good and true and rid this earth of all the evils within it including the evil stockpiles of diseases, inorganic seeds, weapons, clothing, lands and people?

Why continue to suffer at the hands of humans if you truly don't have to?

Let go of the devil's people and let the devil provide for them. Why should you live in shame and disgrace day in and day out whilst humans destroy and kill you at an alarming rate?

Good and true life is true, so why aren't you living true?

Why are you crying due to the ills and sins of humans?

Now tell me, **WHEN DOES YOUR LIFE BEGIN TO MATTER?**

Do you not care about life; the good and true life in you?

Humans create to destroy; kill, and you as Mother Earth permit this to happen. You control the destiny of you and the life in you, but yet you permit and allow wicked and evil humans to destroy and kill you.

You give us the resources for death Mother Earth. Now I ask you this, if humans did not have the resources to destroy and kill, could they kill?

No come on answer me.

You aid and abet humans in their nastiness, so tell me where is your self respect?

Are you not as guilty as Lovey because you give humans the resources to kill and Lovey permit this in every way each and every day?

So are you both not guilty of sin?

So tell me, how can anyone be happy in either of you?

Now I ask you Lovey and Mother Earth this; why do man write, "thou shalt not kill," and both of you kill by permitting death to reside here on earth and take life at will due to sin? Sins the both of you willingly and willfully permit.

So why charge death and humans for sin when the both of you, you Lovey and Mother Earth have and has sinned by permitting it; sins?

So now tell me, if mother and father bask in sin and do sin, will their children not become sinful also? Will we not bask in the delicacies of sin?

So tell me, where is the truth and good justice in either of you, if mother and father hath no good will towards life when it comes to good and true life?

Michelle

Are all things working for you Lovey?

Are you comfortable with the way the world is going right now when it comes to the fighting and disarray of human life on this planet?

ARE YOU TRULY HAPPY THAT THE DEVIL HAS AND HAVE DECEIVED HUMANITY?

Are you truly happy that humans globally worship and praise the devil and or Satan; Death over you Lovey?

Are you happy that nations fight against nations?

Are you happy that his nation is fighting against that nation and killing each other?

Are you truly happy that humans have and has received the calling of evil and are living like the wicked and evil?

Is this the way you truly wanted earth to run and be?

Now tell me, why create if you knew strife would enter the picture and or life at some point in time in life?

Tell me, can a god that truly loves deceive and cause his or her children to live as the deceived?

What good is life is there is truly no truth in it?
What good is a god that cannot truly heal?

What point is life if we as humans cannot live properly and respect each others' values and traditions of cleanliness and truth?

Now tell me Lovey, what good is your life on this earth if no one respects you or even see you as god; the ultimate being?

Do we as humans not idolize man and worship men and women instead of you?

So tell me, how good and true is your life to humans globally?

Did we as humans not make a choice and that choice is truly not you?

It's weird but it's December 05, 2015 and I truly do not feel like writing anymore books for you. I've told you, I have to move on; be on my way because life with you is truly not peaceful nor is it happy. I've been lying to myself and I've bought into the lies of you and I cannot anymore. I need to move on because I am missing so much in life. Things I've let go I cannot get back because of you; meaning my choice to unify with you in goodness and in truth. I also, cannot take the hurt and pain; tears of you anymore. I truly have to think of me and make myself happy because you truly cannot make me happy or truly safeguard me the way I want and need you to. I cannot pretend with you and

I've never pretended with you, but I have to move on in truth. I have to shed the darkness in me and receive true and good life; prosperity all around.

I have to truly find my true happiness and place in life; good and true life, and I cannot do this hanging on to you in a world where I am truly not happy not even with you. **<u>Too much evil is around us; thus the darkness of death comes for billions in society and they don't even know it.</u>**

Let not Death be mine or yours anymore Lovey. I see death and I know death, and I truly want and need to break away from the sight of death. I need a new and true life with you Lovey that is truly clean and I cannot have this where I am Thus I need to truly leave this land and find a truer and cleaner; a more peaceful and harmonious place to live without all these Babylonians; children and people of death for real.

I guess I had too much expectations of you, expectations you cannot nor could you fulfill. I did hurt myself and even though you tried to comfort me, your comfort was truly no comfort to me nor was it healing to me.

Thank you for your effort but you know now just how hard it is to please me. I don't know but maybe, no not maybe, I do expect a lot more from you and like I've said in other books, maybe you just don't have that more to give. You cannot give me what you truly can't and this is sad on my part. I did make you my all, but in the end you could not make me your all. Yes you've shown me many things but yet giving was never your strong point, nor was it a prerequisite in your life. You just cannot give what you can't and I have to accept this.

I have to accept your limitations but in truth, I truly cannot because MY GOD should not be limited and or have limitations. He and yes she should be limitless because you are both.

But it's weird, you are supposed to be the supremest of all, but yet you are flawed like Superman.

You are not all powerful because evil can come in and overthrow you. Thus you are weak and vulnerable just like the earth when it comes to humans. You see the injustice of this planet when it comes to humans globally as well as this earth because it's us as humans that's destroying and killing here and you can't do anything about it. We are the ones that truly do not care about anything when it comes to self preservation and tomorrow; the future. Yes I know you cannot come into a dirty planet and it's our sins that are keeping you away from us, but you know me, I have to blame you for all because I did make you my ALL.

I don't know Lovey because I am on a different mission right now and in true truth, this mission truly does not involve you. You cannot care for people that truly don't care about you. You cannot battle the devil and or sin for us because you did not sin for us, we sinned for self.

Yes I want and need to be on my own and I am slowly moving towards my goal and I am happy. But no, I am not leaving you because in truth, no one can leave your fold if they are secure in you. You truly won't let them and I know this for an indefinite fact.

Yes it's me and maybe now; as of January 01, 2015 true happiness will come my way and I will begin to heal and live again without being restricted and limited in life.

Yes it's Saturday Night and I miss me some good old Zionist Revival. Wow. Watching the Zion roll and my spirit moved. People, your spirit can be truly wonderful, and when it connects to your higher calling it truly connects.

I don't know but there is something I need to do in my life and when I get there I will let you all know.

J. Capri, Ms. Phillips the dance hall artiste has been bugging me, her death I mean. Yu noa when death stings that death is unbelievable; hit you from nowhere. Well this female's death sting, truly sting. Wow. I truly hope the police of Jamaica look into the vehicle because something is truly not right. Shi jus dead soh. Was she speeding?

Did she have a tire blowout?
Did her car brakes fail her?
What truly cause her death because like I said, this death truly stings?

REAL SITUATION

Buoy mi a tell yu, annada hot death. I don't know if any of you can feel the sting of death, but death sting hat wen yu feel it and mi caane tek noh more hat death to yass.

Wow. Hence I am so going to leave this alone because like I said, when death do not want to show you who's going to die sometimes; death masks death and hide the location from you.

People and family, death hat fi some people eeenoa.

Woe, because some of you truly don't know. Unnu truly don't know. Thus those that have eyes truly feel it; the sting of death. Therefore, we are truly not the same and we are plagued by sickness; severe health issues for real.

So yes I was in the spirit today and people I don't know what to make of this. Waking moment visions are truly impossible for me because I truly do not know what they mean. Maybe you can make sense of it.

Saw this beautiful blue river; (think sea water because the water was like sea water). There was this dirt road leading to the river. The road that lead to the river was wide but not too wide. At the mouth of the river; on the left and right hand side of the pathway of the river was tall grass. Tall grass was at the entrance of the river on both sides. This black lady dressed in blue, dark blue and not baby blue was at the entrance way of the river. She had a white waist band on and a white turban on. Under the top part of the dress she had a long sleeve shirt and or sweater on. If you've watched Rastafari Is (the video); the black long sleeve shirt Peter Tosh had on is the same exact shirt she had on under her dress. You could see the black sleeve. I cannot tell you what her face looked like because I could not see her face. She stood at the entrance way of the water on the right hand side if you are walking towards the river. She was just there and as I was in the spirit and seeing her, the water behind her turned black, jet black. She did not move from her position, she was pulling something and you could see this black thing she was pulling from out of me. You can call it webbing, but she did not stop pulling. Could I get close to her?

No, I could not. She kept me at a distance while she was pulling that black thing out of me.

No, truly don't ask me what it is. I know something is inside of me that need to come out. Maybe she is reminding me of this; that I need to get the black thing inside of me out. But how to get it out; I truly do not know.

Michelle

REAL SITUATION

Oh Allelujah why do you let the Babylonians influence so much?

Every language on the face of this planet derives from Babylonian languages and culture, and I have to ask why?

You are not Babylonian, but yet their languages dominate the languages of earth. I know I cannot write your language, but if I could, I would write in your language each and every day. Yes happiness would come because I would be able to heal and pull all facets of evil here on earth as well as in the spiritual realm. But I cannot because I cannot write your language and I am slowly leaving you due to hurt and pain; true abuse of you in the physical and spiritual realm.

Yes I know we are forever ever but forever ever does not mean living in shame and disgrace; an unhealthy environment and dysfunctional relationship.

Maybe one day you will find someone that could endure this pain with you forever ever, but I truly cannot; cannot journey with you on this wicked and evil road anymore. I truly have to think of me and my health and sanity because you are truly not doing so. We had a good run, but I have to lift me up and be happy. The hurt and pain is truly not worth it and the tears are not worth it either. I've had it hard all my life and I cannot continue in this hardship with you any longer. I truly love you, but you have to truly find your way and be truthful to you. You cannot just love so, you have to love true. You have to get over your hurt and pain as well because in truth, you too have baggage, baggage I cannot carry with you any longer. In my book, there is no end to your baggage at all. You do not want to end your hurt and pain; our hurt and pain and I cannot take it anymore. Yes I cuss and get on bad; this is my pain reliever and buster. All I've seen I've shown. All who have hurt me I've let them go forever ever and now it's your turn. I have to let go of your hurt and pain infinitely and indefinitely more than forever ever without end. Like I've said, **truth does not hurt** *and I've been hurt by you constantly.* **And to be totally honest with you and in truth; I make excuses for you and not wanting to leave due to fear and I have to stop this now.** *If you were truly with me you would have seen and known my hurt and pain with you. Like I've said, you are a great protector but a lousy provider and teacher.* **Right can never be wrong Lovey and you need to know this.** *Forgive me for this, but I am going to say it anyway.* **YOU ARE LIKE UNTO SOLOMON. WHEN YOU GET GOOD WOMEN AND OR PEOPLE THAT TRULY LOVE YOU AND ARE TRULY TRUTHFUL TO YOU, YOU DO NOT WANT THEM BECAUSE YOU FIND ALL THE FLAWS IN THE WORLD IN THEM TO PUSH THEM AWAY FROM YOU.**

To you, they have to be your perfect fit of a wurllean, ghetto, and tegareg. They must be fake with the beauty of the world; black widow spider and not of a true and pure heart and I cannot continue with you like this. My heart is pure and clean towards you but yours isn't to me. **So I HAVE TO READ BETWEEN THE LINES AND HAVE AMBITION FOR MYSELF AND TRULY LEAVE YOU ALONE BECAUSE YOU HAVE NO AMBITION AND TRUTH FOR ME.**

If you did, I would not be hurting so much and tears would not come for me in this December month. This month; the month of December I was looking forward to and you took my joy from me. Yes this is you when it comes to me. I get it and see it. I was never the one you truly wanted or needed; thus I have to cut my loss and move on to a better tomorrow for me; self and spirit and yes to a large extent you.

Ah yes, it's December 06, 2015 and all I dreamt about was death. All around me in my dream world is death; Black and White Death. **This is why I ask humanity what are we all fighting for?**

Why are we killing each other and hating based on hue; skin tone and or colour for?

I've told you all time and time again in many of the books in the Michelle Jean series of books; that our skin tone is crap. Stop hating based on skin tone because both colour represent death. **BLACK SKIN TONE REPRESENT PHYSICAL DEATH AND WHITE SKIN TONE REPRESENT SPIRITUAL**

DEATH; THUS THE YING AND YANG ON A DIFFERENT LEVEL.

Thus I was dreaming about Black and White Death.

I also dreamt I was invited to go to a funeral; massive funeral at 3505 Dufferin Street. It's funny the young white female that invited me to the funeral said the intersection was at Keele and Dufferin or was it Dufferin and Lawrence? But in my waking state I was saying; but Keele and Dufferin do not meet. The funeral was set for a certain time and she did not want us to be late because I was with my eldest son. He wanted to go shopping to get something for the funeral but we did not end up going due to time constraints. With us not going shopping this white lady say in her thirties went flowers shopping. I am not sure if it's lilies that were on the flowers tree or plant, but the white lilies I am calling them was on trees; flowers trees and or plants. Some were sagging; withered and some weren't. She did not pick the sagging ones. I don't know what happened to my son but he was not with me anymore and I was helping this young white lady pick flowers. She got a nice bunch of flowers and you could see the green stem of the flowers trees and or stems. It's weird because I've never seen a green flower before and this one tree had one green flower. The flower was green and I said, how about this one and she picked the green flower. Weird

I also dreamt my daughter's friend. I dreamt someone died in her family but I did not see the face of the person. In the

the world; black widow spider and not of a true and pure heart and I cannot continue with you like this. My heart is pure and clean towards you but yours isn't to me. **So I HAVE TO READ BETWEEN THE LINES AND HAVE AMBITION FOR MYSELF AND TRULY LEAVE YOU ALONE BECAUSE YOU HAVE NO AMBITION AND TRUTH FOR ME.**

If you did, I would not be hurting so much and tears would not come for me in this December month. This month; the month of December I was looking forward to and you took my joy from me. Yes this is you when it comes to me. I get it and see it. I was never the one you truly wanted or needed; thus I have to cut my loss and move on to a better tomorrow for me; self and spirit and yes to a large extent you.

Ah yes, it's December 06, 2015 and all I dreamt about was death. All around me in my dream world is death; Black and White Death. **This is why I ask humanity what are we all fighting for?**

Why are we killing each other and hating based on hue; skin tone and or colour for?

I've told you all time and time again in many of the books in the Michelle Jean series of books; that our skin tone is crap. Stop hating based on skin tone because both colour represent death. **BLACK SKIN TONE REPRESENT PHYSICAL DEATH AND WHITE SKIN TONE REPRESENT SPIRITUAL**

DEATH; THUS THE YING AND YANG ON A DIFFERENT LEVEL.

Thus I was dreaming about Black and White Death.

I also dreamt I was invited to go to a funeral; massive funeral at 3505 Dufferin Street. It's funny the young white female that invited me to the funeral said the intersection was at Keele and Dufferin or was it Dufferin and Lawrence? But in my waking state I was saying; but Keele and Dufferin do not meet. The funeral was set for a certain time and she did not want us to be late because I was with my eldest son. He wanted to go shopping to get something for the funeral but we did not end up going due to time constraints. With us not going shopping this white lady say in her thirties went flowers shopping. I am not sure if it's lilies that were on the flowers tree or plant, but the white lilies I am calling them was on trees; flowers trees and or plants. Some were sagging; withered and some weren't. She did not pick the sagging ones. I don't know what happened to my son but he was not with me anymore and I was helping this young white lady pick flowers. She got a nice bunch of flowers and you could see the green stem of the flowers trees and or stems. It's weird because I've never seen a green flower before and this one tree had one green flower. The flower was green and I said, how about this one and she picked the green flower. Weird

I also dreamt my daughter's friend. I dreamt someone died in her family but I did not see the face of the person. In the *dream it is implied that the person was in a body bag. Like I said, the person died. They could not pay to bury the person nor could they keep the body in the morgue. They had to take the body and she my daughter's friend was carrying the dead body home in her hands. She was going to put the dead body beside her and her mother to sleep.*

Yes this is weird thus I am so going to leave these death dreams alone. Just going to watch and see because death could mean marriage, but that's not the case lately with me. I am so not going to read anything into this because these could be dreams in a dream. I can't interpret any more people; too tired of interpreting.

This is the image of the flower in the dream. Stem green but flower was all white. Lily taken from the internet and no copyright infringement intended as picture is used for illustration purpose only.

I don't know if me dreaming about death is due to her being by the river that looked like a sea.

Green they say is disappointment but I truly don't know. So I am so going to leave all these dreams alone.

All I have to say is, we as humans should start living right and put down the hatred and pain because it's truly not worth it. **True life is worth it; thus it's imperative to try to live in the spirit and not in the flesh.**

The spirit is your true life and at the end of the day, THE LIFE YOU LIVE HERE IN THE PHYSICAL (LIVING) DETERMINES WHERE YOU GO IN THE AFTER LIFE AND OR ONCE YOUR SPIRIT SHEDS THE FLESH.

There is a hell and you truly do not want to go there. There is no water in hell and your spirit is dependent on water. Without it; (water), your spirit slowly dies and this is truly what's going to happen to billions of you in hell.

As humans; we forgot that the devil was going to do all to take each and every one of us to hell with him and it matters not how he or she does it. Thus religion and politics is a bitch. Both take you to hell and not one of you knows it.

Lovey and or God is truly not religion, nor does he join in the political arena of death. So truly good luck to many of you the political leaders of the world because your hell is truly not pretty. Many of you dead and living are in hell already. It's just a matter of time before you in the living get there; join the rest that are in hell literally.

Many of you spend billions of dollars to keep death going BUT YET FORGOT ABOUT THE HELL; YOUR HELL THAT YOU ARE GOING TO HAVE TO FACE.

YOU'VE FORGOTTEN THAT IT IS WRITTEN IN YOUR BOOK OF CODES; DEATH THAT, "THOU SHALT NOT KILL." You broke this law and or commandment; thus hell is truly waiting for the lots of you.

And to UGANDA; WHY?

WHY THE HELL WOULD YOU LET THE DEVIL, A KNOWN DEMON INTO YOUR HOLY PLACE?

NO MAN WOMAN OR CHILD THAT MAN ORDAIN IS OF GOOD GOD AND ALLELUJAH; LOVEY AND GOD. COME ON NOW.

NO MAN CARRY THE ORDNANCE OF LOVEY; GOD BECAUSE NONE WAS AND OR IS ORDAINED BY HIM TO CARRY HIS ARK; THE ARK OF THE COVENANT; LIFE. YOU ARE AFRICANS YOU SHOULD KNOW THIS COME ON NOW.

<u>Thus blacks never stop selling self and God out to the devil and the demons of hell. Allelujah</u>

Absolutely no one that is of the church and churches of death represent Life; Lovey, Good God and Allelujah come on now. You should all know this.

<u>ABSOLUTELY NO CHURCH OF LIES AND DECEIT WAS IN THE BEGINNING AND ABSOLUTELY NONE SHALL BE IN THE END. ALLELUJAH; COME ON NOW.</u>

THUS NO ONE THAT IS WICKED AND EVIL; TRULY SINFUL WILL STAND IN THE CONGREGATION OF THE RIGHTEOUS.

<u>IT IS FORBIDDEN AND ALL OF AFRICA SHOULD KNOW THIS BECAUSE MAMA AFRICA IS THE WOMB AND CENTRE OF ALL LIFE COME ON NOW.</u>

REAL SITUATION

KNOW THAT YOUR HOLY PLACE IS NO LONGER HOLY. YOU DEFILED THIS PLACE BY LETTING THE DEVIL; DEMON OF HELL INTO IT.

Your sacred place is now unclean and defiled.

Beg forgiveness and clean it because NO DEMON DUPPY SHOULD HAVE ACCESS TO A HOLY PLACE.

Once filth step foot on or in your holy place, that place becomes corrupt and unclean. YOU ARE AFRICANS AND THE LOTS OF YOU SHOULD KNOW THIS. NO ONE SHOULD ENTER A SACRED PLACE WITH THEIR DIRTY SHOES AND YOU ALL SHOULD KNOW THIS BECAUSE YOU ALL SAY YOU ARE AFRICANS.

Now I ask you this, if you were truly Africans, why are you not doing that which is African?

Why is Africans acting like wurlleans; the deceived?

Africa and or Africans should stop the bullshit that you are all doing. It's time for the lots of you to wake up and stop living like the bleeping dead and destitute. Africa is so rich but yet you're depicted as the carriers of diseases; the infectious disease carriers that inflect the globe with your diseases. **<u>Humans have and has forgotten that many of these diseases were created in laboratories in many European and Western Nations and brought to other lands to kill the inhabitants of that land.</u>**

This is done so that you the European and Western Unions and or Nations can rob them; (other lands), and steal their land and resources. This was done to Africans and still being done to Africans until this day. **<u>THUS YOU PUT IN YOUR BOOK OF CODES; SIN AND DEATH, YOUR SO CALLED HOLY BIBLE THAT GOD WAS BEFORE THE LOTS OF YOU ON THE BATTLEFIELD.</u>**

<u>YES YOUR GOD WHICH IS DEATH WAS BEFORE YOU; THUS THE LOSS OF LIVES; THE LIVES YOU MURDERED; TAKE IN THE NAME OF DEATH.</u>

It's all there in your dirty book called the Holy Bible but yet man cannot put it together; **SO THEY LIE AND SAY GOD, ALLELUJAH, ALLAH, JEHOVAH, JESUS AND WHAT HAVE YOU.**

AND YES WE DI FOOL FOOL BLACK PEOPLE OF THE GLOBE SWEAR UP AND DOWN AND SAY, A SOH, JESUS DIED FOR ME. GOD A GOH WIPE OUT DI DEBBIL.

WE SAY, WHO THAT DON'T BELIEVE IN CHRIST AND ACCEPT THE BLOOD OF CHRIST ARE GOING TO DIE WITHOUT KNOWING THAT YOU (THE CHRISTIANS, MUSLIMS, BAPTISTS, RASTAS, ANGLICANS, CATHOLICS AND WHAT HAVE YOU ARE THE IDIOTS AND FOOLS THAT ARE GOING TO DIE.

IF YOU WE AS AFRICANS AND OTHER NATIONS WERE SO DAMNED TRUTHFUL AND WERE OF AFRICAN DESCENT AND CULTURE; WE WOULD KNOW THAT THERE IS NO JESUS, AND NO ONE CAN DIE TO SAVE YOU. THEY HAVE TO LIVE BY THE TRUTH OF LOVEY AND DO ALL THAT IS TRUTHFUL IN THE LIVING TO SAVE YOU.

WE SAY WE ARE GOD'S PEOPLE, BUT YET BELIEVE AND SAY, INCLUDING TEACH AND PREACH DEATH, THE DEATH OF A MAN. A MAN YOU ALL SAY IS GOD'S CHILD.

IF WE AS HUMAN BEINGS HAD KNOWN LOVEY, GOOD GOD AND ALLELUJAH, WE WOULD HAVE KNOWN THAT HE LOVEY WOULD NEVER EVER SACRIFICE ANY OF HIS AND HER OWN TO SAVE

REAL SITUATION

WICKED AND EVIL PEOPLE; DEATH'S CHILDREN; OWN.

NO REPENTANCE IS GIVEN TO DEATH'S CHILDREN BECAUSE DEATH AND LIFE ARE NOT THE SAME. LIFE IS TRUE TRUTH AND DEATH ARE LIES. THUS HUMANS ARE LIARS, THIEVES AND MURDERERS. WE BELIEVE IN LIES, ACKNOWLEDGE AND PRAISE LIES, AS WELL AS DO WICKED AND SINFUL THINGS.

REPENTANCE IS ONLY GIVEN TO LOVEY'S TRUE OWN. THESE ARE THE PEOPLE THAT LOVEY CAN AND WILL SAVE BECAUSE THEY ARE HIS AND HER OWN. SO I TRULY DON'T KNOW WHY ANYONE WOULD THINK OTHERWISE.

NO EVIL CAN STAND IN THE CONGREGATION OF THE RIGHTEOUS AND WE ALL KNOW THIS. SO WHY WOULD ANY OF YOU SAY THE WICKED AND EVIL WILL BE SAVED?

Lovey's children have and has strayed and it's his people; the true Jews that will be saved and no other.

THERE ARE NO STRAYS THIS TIME AROUND. ONCE ALL IS SAID AND DONE; DEATH WILL AND MUST BE NO MORE BECAUSE NO PLACE IS AND OR IS PROVIDED FOR DEATH AND THEIR PEOPLE.

COME ON NOW YOU SHOULD ALL KNOW THIS.

Yes I know some of you are saying I've converted to Judaism and I am married to a Jew so you're all dancing up and down. Some of you are going to rush out now and get converted to Judaism to be on the safe side. Yeah to the lots of you because you're thinking you are doing right and good to be on the good side of Lovey. Congratulations.

Yeah you!!!!!!!!!!!!!!!

STOP

Stop right there because there is something you truly do not know, and now you are going to know.
<u>Absolutely no one can convert to Judaism.</u>

<u>None!!!!</u>

A Babylonian so called Jew is not a Jew and could never be a Jew; they are Babylonian

because the follow the nasty practice and ways of Abraham the Babylonian.

If these so called Jews; frauds were the true Jews they would know that Abraham was a Babylonian like them.

<u>Wait, they know. This is why you have Death's nasty book, your so called Holy Bible. Thus Revelations say in part, "woe be unto the Jews that call themselves Jews because they are of the synagogue of Satan."</u>

They had to sell you death and bring you to hell with them.

So yes, in many ways I AM TRULY THANKFUL THAT IT WAS NOT BLACK PEOPLE THAT WROTE THIS DECEITFUL, SINFUL, LYING AND DISGUSTING BOOK.

<u>Allelujah, truly thank you for not letting it be us the BLACK RACE THAT WROTE THE BOOK OF DEATH AND DECEIVED BILLIONS. HERE WE DID DO RIGHT AND JUST BY YOU. SO TRULY THANK YOU FOR SAVING US AND SPARING US THE AGONY OF DEATH IN THIS SENSE.</u>

<u>TRULY TRULY THANK YOU WITH A PURE AND CLEAN HEART FOR NOT LETTING US BE THE ONES TO DECEIVE YOU IN THIS WAY; WRITING LIES ABOUT YOU. YOU SAVED US, BUT WE AS BLACK PEOPLE TRULY DO NOT KNOW THIS UNTIL THIS DAY.</u>

Go ahead and say it so I can truly school your ass.

THE ORIGINAL JEWS ARE ETHIOPIANS; THE TRUE BLACK RACE. BUT BECAUSE ETHIOPIA GAVE UP LOVEY, ETHIOPIA IS NO LONGER CONSIDERED A JEWISH NATION AND WILL NEVER BE CONSIDERED A JEWISH NATION AGAIN. THEY THE ETHIOPIANS FORFEITED THEIR TRUE RIGHT AND RIGHTS WITH LOVEY WHEN THEY JOINED BABYLON. THEY WERE THE FIRST TO ABANDON LOVEY THUS THEY ARE INCLUDED IN THE BEGINNING WITH DEATH. AND YES THIS IS WHY REMNANTS OF BLACK PEOPLE CAN BE FOUND IN INDIA UNTIL THIS DAY. AND YES LOVEY HAS A TRUE AND LEGITIMATE BONE TO PICK WITH THEM; ETHIOPIA.

They gave up truth thus YOUR BIBLE TELL YOU ISRAEL; THE JEWS ARE NO MORE.

So because Israel is no more and they forfeited the realm and life of Lovey; successorship fell into the hands of Judah. But the same shit Israel did, Judah did and is doing until this day. Thus many say they have God and or Lovey but in truth, truly do not have him. Lovey truly do not reside with the unclean and deceitful; deceived.

So now; in order for you to be considered a Jew, you have to be chosen by Lovey. You carry his name and truth and you are sealed with truth. Thus the True Jews are not just blacks, some are whites and some are a mixture of white and black.

<u>Yes it's all mixed up due to lies told by men and women including children. The devil had to make it this way. Satan had to make you believe his people are the true Jews when they are truly not.</u>

<u>The devil and his people had to make you bow down to Babylon and the sins of Babylon. They had to make you swear allegiance to all that is of Babylon; all that is sinful and unholy. And every human being globally do so with religion and politics.</u> Religion cannot interfere with politics because they are the Islamic Kingdoms of this world; earth. Thus death cannot go against death nor can death fight against death in this way because they are of the same BLOODLINE. They have the same mother and father literally. <u>But I am hoping that LOVEY WILL WEED OUT THE FAKE JEWS FROM THE REAL JEWS SHORTLY.</u>

The history and or record books of humans are distorted. This had to be because the devil did not want you to know the full truth. The devil had to plant themselves into the equation and this is truly sad and unfair. And yes I did tell you in some of my other books Lovey locks no one out of his kingdom and abode and this truth remains. Like I said time and time again, we are the ones to lock our self out of his kingdom and abode with our sin and sins and this is true.

YOU CANNOT HOLD ON TO LIES. YOU MUST ACCEPT TRUTH AND LIVE BY THE TRUTH IN ORDER FOR YOU TO BE SAVED.

YOU WERE TOLD **"TRUTH IS EVERLASTING LIFE."** This cannot change and will never change.

Yes I know some cannot be saved due to generational sins and some of the sins that we do, but it does not mean you are to give up. Just as the devil and or his people lied to you and concealed the truth, **LOVEY CAN SAY, BECAUSE I SEE THAT YOU HAVE TRIED YOUR BEST AND DONE YOUR BEST TO CLEAN YOURSELF UP IN GOODNESS AND TRUTH, I AM GOING TO EXTEND THE OLIVE BRANCH OF LIFE TO YOU AND LET YOU LIVE. I AM GOING TO SAVE YOU BECAUSE YOU RECOGNIZED YOUR FAULTS AND YOU DID COME TO ME IN TRUTH FOR A SAVING GRACE. YOU DID TRY TO MAKE YOURSELF CLEAN; WHOLE.**

Strayed

As Africans you are shown as poor and living in rat infested dung holes begging and waiting for a hand out from Western and Eastern Civilizations. So tell me, where has all the original African Civilizations and Empire gone?
Have you forgotten that when you dance with the devil you get burned?

Have you forgotten that the origin of life is black and or the foundation of life is black, and no one is going to truly like you because of jealousy?

No this has nothing to do with skin tone but has all to do with life and the existence of life. Thus no one comprehends the light in the darkness because in truth, no one can see the true light of life in them; within the darkness of life and this universe.

So yes, I am slowly becoming done with Lovey and the Universe and soon to be Earth. In truth and to me and only me, Earth has no respect of person; self, thus she too has and have allowed her domain to be infected with rodents; humans that destroy and kill her; all life everywhere.

Michelle

It's weird Lovey but what am I to you?

Am I not slowly moving away from you due to hurt and pain; dissatisfaction and injustice on your part, as well as the part of this earth?

Listen Lovey and God; Good God and Allelujah, I am truly not getting involved with you and Russia. Yes there are lies circulating and you kept drilling truth in my head in my dream state and Russia was at the forefront.

I truly do not know what lies they are telling, but I am truly not going to let it concern me anymore. I've shed my tears already and humanity has to pay the price for their lies and deceit; their destroying and killing agenda. Death is their agenda and I am truly stepping aside from you and humanity including this world; earth, the spiritual realm, you and the universe.

What men do to self no longer concerns me. War and strife is their mainstay thus their devilish agenda here on earth. Each and every one of us see the issues and problems here on this earth and or in this planet and instead of outing the fire many continue to escalate it. So no, Russia and their lies concern me not because at the end of the day, every human being and sub human must pay according to their evil and deceitful works; agenda.

What death do to humanity no long concern me. I am tired of the lies; thus I've told you time and time again, that I do not want or need a weak god. **_I truly love strength and power and to me you are weak. You've let death defeat you and man, so tell me, where was your strength in all of this? Death infiltrated your home, took your people, used them to spread hate and lies; then death turned around and mocked you by putting their people at the forefront of it all whilst lambasting you and glorifying themselves here on earth and in your presence._** *Death's children built churches and statues of so called saints; men and women and say they are of you when they are truly not of you, but of death. All that is dirty and unclean humans and animals feast on; cleanliness was never in the equation of life when it came to you and men, thus the unclean and dirty book (Holy Bible) men wrote and say it is of you. Truth and cleanliness is my mainstay.*

You are my mainstay because I do truly think of you and I truly want and need what is good and best for you. Lies and deceit isn't in our equation; thus truly do not bring it (lies) to me or give it (lies) to me. Good and true life need to be preserved and lived; thus earth need to be cleaned of the filth that man; humans and sub humans leave in her.

Perversions of sin men strive on and or for to the point where men; humans say it is lawful by you to have more than one wife.

Man marry family member.
Man seek pleasure with the innocent including children and all of this you Lovey see and know but yet are

REAL SITUATION

powerless to do anything about it. Thus I've told you, you are weak and powerless when it comes to cleaning up earth. Humans should not class you as low and defiled as them, but you let it happen anyway. Yes, thus the different gods and goddesses humans praise and worship; put above you.

Death made earth his and her stronghold; thus governments are run and overseen by wicked and evil men and women that have no true respect for life and the preservation of life.

They break the law and laws of life each and every day and you wonder why earth is this messed up and jacked up. Lovey, life has no worth here on earth anymore. Life isn't regarded. Just look at the gangs of earth that take like at will for death.

<u>**Earth isn't truthful anymore because humans have and has turned this planet into the planet of death. Thus humans build spaceships; rocket to travel to other planets to spread their germs; diseases of hate and strife; war. Everywhere death goes death kills. Humans are death because they carry death with them everywhere they go and humans do kill come on now; you and I know this.**</u>

So no, with all I see here on earth; I truly do not want to proceed with you any longer in a dirty and unclean state. The injustice and death toll of humans is too much for me to bear. Yes I want and need death's wicked and evil children gone from this world but in truth, they cannot leave because they own earth. They give the command of who lives and who dies. You Lovey are powerless in doing anything because you are truly not here on this earth. You do not have to face and see the ordeals; sufferings of humans each and every day. Humans cry out yes and they feel they are crying out to you but in truth, they cannot cry to you because you have nothing to do with us due to sins; the sins of the fathers and mothers that have been handed down from generation to generation and more. I have debts that need to be repaid and you cannot help me to repay them and I've come to realize this.

You made me cry Lovey and I am truly hurt by this. I did not have to cry in December and the month has just begun. So no more. You want to continue with man; humans, then continue with them but our journey with each other is coming to an end slowly.

I need to be in an environment that is void of cheaters, liars, murderers, scammers, warmongers, whores and prostitutes, pedophiles, gang members of death, diseases of men and spirit, unclean water and house, unclean homes and gods, children and family including others and much much more. Life didn't have to be dirty, but we as humans dirtied it then have the Gaul to cry out and or call out to you Lovey for a saving grace. Call out to the god and gods including goddesses you all put over Lovey. You have no care and respect for Lovey but yet you have the nerve to want him to save you. You trample him down and he's to turn a blind eye and say, John, Rueben, Telisha, Veronica, Michelle, Stacey, Ben, Fred, Ron, Danny, it's okay, I'll save you even though you did not choose me.

Wow

Amazing the hypocrites and parasites we've become; are.

We all want to do all to be happy no matter the consequence; who we hurt. So we hurt self and others including the god we claim to love. We have no regard for life and now that we've reached critical mass; we want to be saved from the willful sins we've committed.

I need a rich and balanced life where I am truly happy and helpful in a positive way each and every day.

I truly don't need the hurt of you and anyone anymore. Thus I've told you Lovey, I cannot live in an unclean environment not even with my children. They don't clean and given my yoyo health issues; I cannot continue on with them. They truly don't help me when it comes to the upkeep of the home we live in. When I ask for help; I am being told no, and some say they will and until now they cannot do. It's way too hard for me and in truth; I truly do not want or need to be in this country. Like I've said time and time again, you keep us in environments we truly do not want to be in. It's as if we are tied to one place and it's pissing me off to know that you as God hinder your people.

You allow other people to steal our life and true life story by saying it's theirs. I've told you about this and nothing is truly being done on your part about it. Thus when you asked me to write, I was only writing in vain. Thus recently I've told you, I want nothing from you because mi dyam out a audda. When I turn from someone or something; I truly turn from them and you Lovey as God; Good God and Allelujah is truly no exception to the rule in my book. I cannot walk in vain with a God that would rather have humans destroy it all for the rest of civilization.

So tell me, if you were truly the right and good god for all, why are your people crying out to you in vain?

Why do you not truly answer your good and true own?

You left us to die at the wayside and in truth; that is truly not fair and just on your part all around.

I cannot stay in lies and in an unhealthy relationship with anyone because the hurt and pain is too great. So truly do not draw me into your beef with Russia; I am truly not having it anymore. You have beef and strife with Russia; use a Russian to deliver your message, they speak the language and are of the Russian culture and truly leave me out of it. I am not being disrespectful, but our journey is slowly coming to an end. What Russia do to secure their people and future is truly not up to me because in truth; they are not my people.

Humans have and has made their choice and I've told you Lovey and God; Good God and Allelujah that choice was truly not you. Humans chose death over you. Death was their choice and you have to leave them; humanity alone. Yes you've done that; left us, but in doing this; you did not truly secure your good and true own and this is where and why I fight with you so.

You cannot show me the magnitude of loving so and leave your good and true own to die at the hands of the wicked and evil. You and Mother Earth are wrong in giving evil and wicked people a home. **<u>Mother Earth is obligated to life and so are you Lovey, but it seems the only life the both of you are obligated to is Death and keeping death alive.</u>** *Thus good and true life has and have become a joke here on earth. Thus I truly do not need a weak god and earth. I need to feel strength and neither you Lovey and earth are strong anymore. You're not strong enough for me. Sad yes, but true in my book for now. You (Lovey and Earth) are both the defeated because in truth; death did defeat all including the both of you.*

Death stole and conquered; colonized and destroyed and there wasn't a damned thing either one of you could do. Thus strength and power is truly not given to the weak and fearful, it is given to the strong and fearless; the wicked and evil heathens of this earth. Men and women who form alliances with death to deceive and kill. So truly don't tell me about truth and justice because I see no truth and justice in this earth. All I see are murderers and thieves that create laws to protect their evil own. Some even go as far as saying; these laws are from you Lovey and until this day you've done nothing to change this and or bring down this blatant lie on the part of humans; men and women including children.

And truly don't go there with disobedience because you did go against the good and true code of life when you created Will and gave it to man.

Yes you did not take away our right to choose, but you should have never put a negative grain in your book and creation.

You knew just how powerful negative energy is and when let loose, negative energy absorb all that is good and true whilst leaving destruction and death; total darkness in its path. You knew the real situation before hand and ignored it. So yes I will continue to blame you for this. Good should never ever have anything to do with evil period. So on this part you failed me just as I've failed you in some areas of my life.

You Lovey knew the consequences, but yet ignored it (the consequences). You cannot give uncivilized people power and strength, but yet you went ahead and did it anyway.

REAL SITUATION

You knew humans are uncivilized beings that cannot live in a peaceful environment. Their brain capacity could not and cannot over stand the spiritual realm. They know not beauty and true peace; so how the hell do you expect them to live in true peace here on earth? For them it's survival, consumption, greed, gratification and not preservation and maintenance. **<u>LOVEY, IF A MAN OR WOMAN INCLUDING CHILD KNOW NOT LIFE, HOW DO YOU EXPECT THEM TO LIVE LIFE?</u>**

If a man or woman including child know not truth, how the hell do you expect them to live by the truth of life; All?

If we know not Allelujah, how the hell do you expect us to say Allelujah and cry out to All; Allelujah?

Yes I know the consequences of sin Lovey and so do you, but when it's all said and done, you too are to blame for negligence and lies; sin and sins.

You as God and All have a long way to go and it's a shame that we had to come to an end like this, but you too need to listen to the true and genuine cries of the few that wanted to get to know you truthfully.

You cannot give in vain Lovey.
You cannot give deceitfully.

You cannot abandon the ones that need to be truthful forever ever with you. But as I've come to learn, you are truly not forever ever. You sit at the wayside and watch as the wicked and evil take it all from you and your children and destroy it all. Thus I truly will not get involved with you and Russia because you did give humans Will like I've said. If humans want to be lied to, it's their decision. We made that choice without consulting you.

In all that humans have done, death was always their choice and I've told you this time and time again.

Whatever problem you have with Russia when it comes to lies and deceit, you resolve it with them because I am so out. I refuse to get involved in an area that I know nothing about. Well I refuse to know. If humans want to kill themselves well so be it. Let them die because life is not worth it to billions. **<u>Russia should know you cannot bargain with the devil. No one that bargains with the devil is a victor.</u>** Just look at the state and economy of **THE UNITED STATES OF AMERICA. You will forever be in debt to sin. All and or the majority of your financial resources must go towards keeping death alive; thus America has a military budget of over $700 billion while the majority of their over 363 million people are hungry, dying of want and need; food, shelter and medicine.**

So no, Lovey what a government do to secure themself with death is truly up to them and not me or you. **The**

choice and or decision was made to follow death and you as God have to live with this decision. Life is not the choice of humans so get over it. *You do not hang on to your good and true own Lovey. No, that's a lie because despite what I write you hang on to me. You keep me out of environments that are truly not clean. So I give you that much. But Russia you truly have to deal with on your own. I am also thinking warmth Lovey. Can our warmth combined warm a heart that is truly cold and not true?*

Truly look at the real situation and see earth as well. Earth is just an arena filled with liars and thieves, liars and thieves that value not life or the truth of life. Earth has and have become the dung of the universe; hence murderers and thieves are jailed here and kept from other planets.

Humans seek to pollute and destroy; thus the universe protect other planets from us; the inhabitants of this earth, whilst scientist lie to humans saying they can see into the life of other planets. Please!!! I can't see into the life of other planets a part from the planet of death. So if I can't see into the life of other planets with my true spiritual eye, what makes scientists any different; true?

Humans are a bleeping joke; thus the universe lock us out and or distort the way to other planets. We talk about technology but humans have not the technology to travel to other solar systems.
We talk about gravity and space ships but yet truly do not know about vibe; vibration. So humans can kiss my ass

with their junk; space tales and lies. You know what let me stop. With all the black holes in space; I know humans have not the technology to travel to another planet; not even the moon, thus tell lie vision (television) is so important to the lies of man period. Therefore movies tell the tales of human lies all around period. The devil and their people are master liars thus they own tell lie vision.

Evil needed a gimmick Lovey and you were the gimmick; thus the so called holy bible of lies that was written by men. Wicked and evil men that brainwash humanity into thinking they have a saving grace when they knew they had none; have none.

So tell me, what new world order is humanity talking about when we already live in man's world order of lies and deceit?

This platform or foundation was always the order of death. It cannot get any worse because we bought into the realm of death and death must come. Death is inevitable not just for the poor and destitute but for the rich and elite as well. Humans did the bidding of death and we are all going to get paid and that payment is death. We were told, "THE WAGES OF SIN IS DEATH." So as humans continue to sin, death continue to come. Death must get paid. Hence we as humans made ourselves sacrifices unto death for real.

Michelle

Another day has dawn and I truly don't know what truth I am missing. Maybe it's the fact that I am slowly leaving Lovey and he's reminding me of my commitment to him. **<u>But I say unto him, how can anyone keep their vow and or commitment to him living in exile?</u>**

How can anyone keep their vow and or commitment to him surrounded by wickedness and evil?

Good should not live side by side with evil and this is my take. In my view right now; there should have never been a Blue and White Nile because despite having this, there is absolutely no peace here on earth.

Yes, I saw the true peace out of the darkness; blackness of life and had to wonder what we as humans are truly fighting for? I felt this peace, but yet humans do not know this true peace. Human cannot comprehend peace; true peace. Thus we live like savages whist saying we are civilized. We talk about cavemen of old, but humans today are no different from the cavemen of old. We are barbaric thus humans live to kill and destroy. No wonder other civilizations hide from us; don't want to be tainted by us.

In a civil society there is no lawlessness.
There is no power struggle.
There's no death and dishonour.

There's no control.
No brutality.

*No disloyalty.
No killing.*

All there is is true peace and harmony in a balanced and fair; just system. There are no set of laws and rules for this culture and that culture; race and or ethnicity. This is a free society where life; good and true life is the prime objective. All is one with nature and nature is one with all.

Everyone is free because everyone have good and true life; freedom.

There are no ethnicity because the spirit cannot and will never partake in lies; the lies of men by dividing us into races and or ethnic groups. The spirit cannot do this because the spirit belongs not to a tribe or ethnic group. The spirit is free, but yet on earth it's held captive and prisoner by the flesh due to sin our sins and the sins of others that surrounds us.

In a civil society we work together as one unified spirit to ensure true balance and harmony in our society. We are a true family that seek the best interest of all. Yes to some this is a fantasy world, but is it truly?

Do not the wicked and evil seek to control all? If they cannot control you and bring you their way; they destroy and kill you including the land and or environment you live in? Look at the world today and tell me if this isn't happening? Are you living in a balanced society; system?

Do you have freedom to travel from this land to the next?

Are you a global citizen?

Do you have a global passport that is void of all restrictions, restrictions imposed on you by so called governments; wicked and evil men and women that dominate and control our god given life?

Are we not restricted and told we cannot enter this land or that land?

You see and know the real situation of earth, and instead of laying down arms; we bear arms and kill each other. We kill each other for something we truly cannot get. At the end of the day we are going to die and leave it all behind. So what is all the fighting for?

Instead of living our lives good and true, we die to go to hell and face a more brutal hell.

I see the real situation of humans on this earth and to be honest with you now; I truly don't care who lives or who dies because we are truly not good people. We say we are good but yet governments invests heavily in death and not life; good and true life.

Governments build machines to kill.
Create diseases to wipe out nations.

Conquer and steal.
Defile and distort the law and laws of good and true life.

Now tell me, why should I care or God; Good God and Allelujah, Lovey even care?

The real situation of earth has nothing to do with God but man and our inability to get along and live good with each other.

Therefore, I've come to the conclusion that no one can live good in an unclean society. No matter how hard you try to be good and do good, you fail because the surroundings you are in and or living in is unclean; evil.

Good cannot live with evil because good becomes unclean once evil and or an unclean person come into your fold and realm; surroundings. ALL YOUR GOODNESS IS DESTROYED BECAUSE EVIL AND OR NEGATIVE FORCES DESTROY AND KILL ALL AROUND; THIS I'VE COME TO KNOW. Thus I've come to the realization that the good seeds Lovey has and have given me cannot be planted on earth or in the hearts of man; humans, because our hearts are truly not true nor are they pure. I can ask and ask but it cannot be done given the real situation; dirty state of this earth; humans.

Yes this is sad but yet; why did he Lovey ask me for a Mega Mansion here on earth?

REAL SITUATION

I have to question the validity of his asking because in truth; he cannot come back to a dirty planet. He's locked out but yet he wants a house here. This makes no sense to me on this day. Thus life is a learning process for me each and every day.

Yes it's December 7th and I dreamt Shaq. He had no tattoos yeah me. I can't remember if he was playing basketball; all I know was he was in pain. His joints were acting up and I went to get A5 35 to rub on his knee. Weird because I'd let Shaq go because of his affiliation with Free Masonry. Wow

Thus dreams and or my dream world is wow. In some way you can say dreams are an alternate universe; our gateway to a parallel universe. Dreams are a reflection of life; our life in some way due to Will and or the Ying and the Yang. You see life and you see death; more death than life and it scary at times but you overcome it.

No, you can't give up. You just have to press on and more on the best you can.

So with all I've learned; there is one thing I know, and this one thing is stressed time and time again in my dream world. That one thing is truth; goodness and truth. One cannot live a clean life without truth. Thus we were told, **"TRUTH IS EVERLASTING LIFE."**

In life you have to be committed to truth.
You have to live by the truth and cleanliness of life.

REAL SITUATION

You have to live a good, true and honest life.

No one can live happy in a dirty and or unclean home. The dirt of your home bogs you down thus billions of us live in an unclean world. Therefore, this earth is infested by and or with, cockroaches, rats, mice, humans of the wicked and evil kind; dirty kind. This earth is infested with, unclean beasts and more including the devils and or demons of the spiritual realm that some humans worship. Demons and devils like the cow and pig; fire and the dead that some use in their voodoo or obeah rituals. Thus this morning's conversation I had with Lovey on a different level.

No one, absolutely no one can say they are clean living in an unclean world not even me. Anyone say they are clean I have to ask; what makes them clean?

What makes me clean?

From your house is dirty you are dirty.
From the environment you live in is dirty; you are dirty also.

We say cleanliness is next to godliness, so why are we not living clean and doing all that is clean in the sight of God? Come on now. What makes us clean if we pollute; dirty our waterways and life itself?

WE SAY LIFE, BUT TRULY DO NOT GIVE LIFE A CHANCE. We know not life come on now.

WE SAY GOD BUT TRULY DO NOT LIVE BY GOD OR HIS RULES; LAWS.

We know not God so we cannot live for him nor can we live by his rules; laws.

WE SAY GOOD OVER EVIL, BUT YET WE DO NOT LIVE GOOD. WE LIVE FOR ALL THAT IS WICKED AND EVIL.

WE CREATE EVIL SYSTEMS AND EVIL SOCIETIES TO CONTROL AND DESTROY; KILL. SOCIETIES THAT PIT NATION AGAINST NATION; HUMAN AGAINST HUMAN.

So absolutely nothing that humans do is about good and true life. So if we nothing that is good and true; how can God and or Lovey truly save us in the end?

Michelle

And for those of you who are wondering if I am going to go back into church because of the black woman in blue and white by the sea like river.

The answer is truly no. No matter how she pulled me, I cannot return to church. I saw the darkness of the water behind her and the church is no where I want and need to be. Psalms One people. Despite me slowly leaving Lovey and him reminding me of my vow and or marriage to him. I cannot disappoint him nor can I disrespect him in this way. Like I said in Our Journey/My Anger, I am leaving the pain and hurt that I feel behind and not him. Our vow (all who are chosen by Lovey), our vow to him is in sickness and in health. Many of us start on the sickness stage and I'm pretty sure I told you this in another book. We see a lot and go through a lot but it's only for a time. I know release come for me and I am truly hoping it's soon; well before 2016. I truly need to live a good, clean, harmonious, pure and truthful life including truly loving and giving.

So as we usher in 2016 shortly; I truly hope all will be truly well and good with me and Lovey including you from now on. Hey, maybe I won't be so lonely. Maybe I can start a new phase in life where I travel extensively for the betterment of not just me but you. Truly hoping I can take some of you to some of the places I go if it is permitted.

Michelle

OTHER BOOKS BY MICHELLE JEAN

Blackman Redemption – The Fall of Michelle Jean
Blackman Redemption – After the Fall Apology
Blackman Redemption – World Cry – Christine Lewis
Blackman Redemption
Blackman Redemption – The Rise and Fall of Jamaica
Blackman Redemption – The War of Israel
Blackman Redemption – The Way I Speak to God
Blackman Redemption – A Little Talk With Man
Blackman Redemption – The Den of Thieves
Blackman Redemption – The Death of Jamaica
Blackman Redemption – Happy Mother's Day
Blackman Redemption – The Death of Faith
Blackman Redemption – The War of Religion
Blackman Redemption – The Death of Russia
Blackman Redemption – The Truth
Blackman Redemption – Spiritual War
Blackman Redemption – The Youths
Blackman Redemption – Black Man Where Is Your God?

The New Book of Life
The New Book of Life – A Cry For The Children
The New Book of Life – Judgement
The New Book of Life – Love Bound
The New Book of Life – Me
The New Book of Life – Life

Just One of Those Days
Book Two – Just One of Those Days
Just One of Those Days – Book Three The Way I Feel
Just One of Those Days – Book Four

The Days I Am Weak
Crazy Thoughts – My Book of Sin
Broken
Ode to Mr. Dean Fraser

A Little Little Talk
A Little Little Talk – Book Two

Prayers
My Collective
A Little Talk/A Time For Fun and Play
Simple Poems
Behind The Scars
Songs of Praise And Love

Love Bound
Love Bound – Book Two

Dedication Unto My Kids
More Talk
Saving America From A Woman's Perspective
My Collective the Other Side of Me
My Collective the Dark Side of Me
A Blessed Day
Lose To Win
My Doubtful Days – Book One

My Little Talk With God
My Little Talk With God – Book Two

A Different Mood and World – Thinking

My Nagging Day
My Nagging Day – Book Two

Friday September 13, 2013
My True Love
It Would Be You
My Day

A Little Advice – Talk
1313, 2032, 2132 – The End of Man
Tata

MICHELLE'S BOOK BLOG – BOOKS 1 – 22

My Problem Day
A Better Way
Stay – Adultery and the Weight of Sin – Cleanliness
Message

Let's Talk
Lonely Days – Foundation
A Little Talk With Jamaica – As Long As I Live
Instructions For Death
My Lonely Thoughts
My Lonely Thoughts – Book Two
My Morning Talks – Prayers With God
What A Mess
My Little Book
A Little Word With You
My First Trip of 2015
Black Mother – Mama Africa
Islamic Thought
My California Trip January 2015
My True Devotion by Michelle – Michelle Jean
My Many Questions To God
My Talk
My Talk Book Two

My Talk Book Three – The Rise of Michelle Jean
My Talk Book Four
My Talk Book Five
My Talk Book Six
My Talk Book Seven
My Talk Book Eight – My Depression
My Talk Book Nine – Death
My Talk Book Ten – Wow
My Day – Book Two
My Talk Book Eleven – What About December?
Haven Hill
What About December – Book Two
My Talk Book Twelve – Summary and or Confusion
My Talk Book Thirteen
My Talk Book Fourteen – My Talk With God
My Talk Book Fifteen – My Talk
My Thoughts – Freedom
My Heart to Heart With Lovey – God

Letters to my song and words of praise and truth; My true and unconditional Love; Lovey, Good God and Allelujah

Caged
Why
I Don't Know But I Know
Our Journey/ My Anger